Our Beautiful Universe

A Young Astronomer's Guide To Stars, Planets, Constellations and More

By Vivian Zitek

First edition, 22nd June 2021. All rights reserved. © Vivian Zitek

Contents

From exploding stars to the black holes that they create, which consume everything in their path, the cosmos can be a chaotic place! There are stars which weigh more than our whole solar system and planets that have never even been lit by a sun.

Space is vast, though, and there are also peaceful sights. The planets offer a palette of colors wrapping their surfaces. Colorful strands of nebulae and the silhouette of colossal dust clouds paint the deepest reaches of the cosmos. There is no corner of the universe that isn't touched by beauty!

Depending on where you live, a good night will grant you the view of thousands of stars! Every one of those points of light is a gigantic ball of plasma fueled by hydrogen. With some of them large enough to fill our whole solar system, it's a wonder that they appear so tiny to us in the sky. That's because they are unfathomably far away from us, with the closest one taking four light years to get to!

That's not all, though! If you're lucky you may just see a planet hanging in the sky, or a shooting star flying by. Further up north or down south some people even get to see the auroras of Earth. The brightest of anything in the night sky is right in our cosmic backyard: The Moon! So, what exactly is there to see, where can you see it, and how do you see it?

Seeing the Cosmos
Naked-eye Astronomy

When you look up to the night sky without any kind of telescope it's called "naked-eye astronomy". Many wonders of the cosmos rely on our ability as humans to see the bigger picture. It may not seem as rewarding as a telescope, but there's actually many things you can only do with the naked eye! What you can see all depends on how bright an object is. Let's take a look and shed some light on the scale and a little trick to see even more!

Objects in the night sky have different levels of brightness that we call magnitude. Strangely, the scale works backwards to what you would think. Lower numbers are brighter and higher numbers are dimmer. The brightest star in the sky, Sirius, has a magnitude of -1.46! This is almost twice as bright as the second brightest star, Canopus.

In comparison, the Sun is considerably dimmer at a magnitude of -27! This is so bright for us though that when all the light hits the atmosphere it blocks out every single star in the sky. If it were dimmer you'd be able to see the other constellations during day time.

There is a limit to how much you can see, however, even under perfect conditions. This is typically put at around a magnitude of 6.5, comparable to the brightness of the planet Uranus at its very dimmest.

A good test you can do is look for the Triangulum Galaxy in the constellation Triangulum! Under a good dark sky, you can see it as a fuzzy patch in the sky, as if a star had been smudged.

Brighter still is the famous Andromeda Galaxy. On a moonless night it can be seen even where the sky has been dulled out by city light. It's fantastic to think that when you look at it your eyes are directly seeing an entire galaxy which is millions of light years away!

If you have trouble seeing them though, don't worry! There's still a trick that you can use which takes advantage of the eye itself. It's called your averted vision! When an object seems a bit too dim or seems to disappear when you look directly at it there's a simple fix: Look slightly to the side of it while continuing to pay attention to it. A little practice goes a long way and remember that some directions may work better than others.

Earth-Based Telescopes
Not everything can be seen with the naked eye, of course. So, we invented telescopes to help us see even deeper into the cosmos. The three most common types of personal telescopes are refractors, reflectors, and catadioptrics. If that last one seems daunting don't worry, all three are based on simple concepts which we'll explain.

Refracting telescopes have been around since the time of Galileo, he used one to spot and track the four biggest moons of Jupiter. They are constructed with a large main lens that takes in and concentrates starlight! When you focus it even further with an eyepiece you get a closer view of the night sky.

Reflectors do the same thing except that they use mirrors! A large, curved mirror reflects light onto a smaller one. This light then travels through the eyepiece to be straightened out and viewed.

Although it sounds complicated, the word catadioptric is just the combination of the Ancient Greek words for "mirror" and "lens"; The telescope is just that! When a main lens and a curved mirror are combined it makes a compound telescope with the benefit of being shorter than either type.

The biggest drawback of a reflector is that it needs a huge piece of glass to work. That weight adds up quickly! To get bigger telescopes we use delicately made mirrors which are installed into observatories.

Wavelengths of the Cosmos
So far we've talked about what we can see with visible light. But what about everything else? Light comes in a wide variety of wavelengths, which are all categorized on the electro-magnetic spectrum! From radio waves on the longest end to gamma rays on the shortest end, each type plays a role in how we understand the universe.

We use radio waves for sending out all kinds of information. An important feature of them is their ability to bounce off the atmosphere, travelling world-wide. Communication, music, radio shows, and satellites all rely on this part of the spectrum. They're also emitted by many kinds of cosmic objects. One of the most fascinating of these are quasars which were actually discovered using radio waves!

Microwaves are next and they're used for more than just heating food. One of the most important things they do is power GPS signals! They can't travel far, but their lack of bouncing means that they're perfect for direct communication! Most of all though, they allow us to see what the birth of the universe was like in the cosmic microwave background radiation.

When you feel the Sun on your skin or the warmth from a heat lamp you're feeling infrared radiation. This wavelength sits just below the color red and is produced by anything that gives off heat. Dust clouds in space block the view of regular telescopes, but they allow infrared to pass which makes it perfect for seeing hidden stars. The biggest downside is that because of all the infrared sources on Earth, most telescopes have to be in space to work.

The human eye works by picking up visible light, our thin slice of the spectrum. Almost all life depends on these wavelengths to survive and the ones that don't evolved from creatures that did. This is the one type of astronomy that has existed for as long as we've looked up to the stars.

Black lights, sunblock, and glowing rocks all rely on ultraviolet light. The Sun puts out an enormous amount of ultraviolet light which is dangerous to living things, luckily our atmosphere blocks most of it out! That makes it tricky for astronomy from the surface though. Telescopes viewing areas of hot star formation must instead be in the upper atmosphere or in space.

X-rays help us uncover some of the most mysterious parts of the cosmos. The most fascinating of which has to be dark matter! It emits no light, has no electric charge, and only interacts through gravity. But some models suggest that it could occasionally give off x-rays, giving us a way to study it!

At the top of the chart are gamma rays! Whether from black holes shredding stars apart or from monstrous solar flares, gamma rays are produced by the most powerful events in the universe. That says a lot for nuclear explosions which also give off intense flashes of gamma rays.

Space Telescopes

We see with visible light because that's what the atmosphere primarily lets through. That's great for us, but not so much for telescopes here on the ground trying to see other wavelengths. Problems rarely stop us though so to solve this one we sent telescopes to space!

Lined up as the next generation of space telescopes is the James Webb Space Telescope, affectionately known as "Webby". It will be bigger and better than the famous Hubble Space Telescope, allowing us to see further and learn more about the universe.

We can also expect to see the Laser Interferometer Space Antenna (LISA) launched in the 2030s. The three probes that make it up will orbit the Sun, forming a triangle with sides nearly twice as long as the Sun itself! It will detect gravitational waves which can be produced by the merging of black holes.

Later still in the late 2030s is the planned Large Ultraviolet Optical Infrared Surveyor (LUVOIR). With a segmented mirror over twice as big as Webby it will pierce the cosmos in search of exoplanets!

Star Light, Star Bright

Sorting the Stars

All stars are placed somewhere on the H-R Diagram which gives them a specific spectral type. These types are O, B, A, F, G, K, M, L, and T. It's strange that the order is so jumbled, isn't it? Well there's a good reason for that which would stand to shape how we view stars all the way to today!

The spectra of a star is based on which elements in it give off light. This light is caused by the intense heat that the elements are under which excites them and gives off photons. Different temperatures cause different photons to be given off, which we can measure and classify.

Annie Cannon was an astronomer who worked with Edward Pickering to classify the stars in the sky. The stars were originally sorted by the strength of their hydrogen spectra from A to Q. Cannon kept these letters but instead arranged these types in order of their temperature. The left-over letters were then used to classify stars outside the normal range, nebulae, and novae.

Spectral Types

The temperature of a star directly determines its color based on blackbody radiation. A blackbody is something that absorbs all light that hits it; In other words, the only light that comes from it is what it emits. Although stars are not perfect blackbodys, they're close enough that we can use the relationship between heat and light to classify them.

All the way at the bottom of the list are T- and L-type stars. These two represent brown dwarfs! These cosmic objects aren't quite stars but they aren't planets either, instead filling their own niche. Compared to stars they give off very little heat with some being as cold as your body temperature. This also means that very little light is given off and makes them tough to spot.

Holding the majority of stars in the night sky are M-types. This mainly includes red dwarfs but also describes most supergiant stars! Although red supergiants have similar temperatures to red dwarfs, they are much larger and produce more light. Red dwarfs are low-mass stars, like brown dwarfs, but they have enough pressure to fuse hydrogen into helium, producing energy.

K-type stars are similar to M-types and have dwarfs as well as giants. A good example of these stars is the second closest star to our Sun, Alpha Centauri B in the constellation Centaurus! Because of its size it isn't bright enough to see with the naked eye. This isn't the case for the K-type giant Arcturus in Boötes, though!

Although they're typically called yellow stars, G- and F-type stars are almost all white! Our own Sun is a perfect example of a G-type star. It appears yellow to us through the atmosphere but in space it shows its true colors, literally. For F-types we have Procyon in the constellation Canis Minor, the little dog. What appears as one star is actually two stars orbiting each other with one orbit taking 41 years!

Sirius, the brightest star in the sky, is a perfect example of an A-type star. While these stars are some of the most common seen by the naked eye, they lack the means of emitting x-rays and don't show up on x-ray surveys.

Ranking in as the hottest stars in the universe are B- and O-type stars! B-type stars can have temperatures as high as six times that of the Sun while O-types can get even hotter. Both types are rare but because of their brightness they can easily be seen over astronomically long distances.

Naming the Stars
Some stars have particular names while others are just Greek letters and numbers. What's up with that? Like many things in astronomy, it comes down to brightness and human culture.

Hearing names like Alpha Centauri and Gamma Corvi may sound like sci-fi words thrown together, but they actually hold useful information! The first part of the name is a Greek letter which is chosen based on brightness. For example, alpha being the first letter shows that the star is the brightest in a constellation.

The name used after the letter is the constellation that the star is in. Corvi means that the star is in Corvus, the crow. While Centauri means it's in Centaurus, the centaur. This kind of naming is called a Bayer designation.

Many stars will have a number instead of a Greek letter. But rather than brightness, then number is based on the star's position in the constellation. This kind of naming is called a Flamsteed designation.

Brightness and position aren't all that matter, though. Culture and history have been important in naming the brightest stars in the sky. Most of these stars come from either Latin, Greek, or Arabic and reflect those cultures.

Constellations

We often see pictures and shapes in groups of bright stars, these are called constellations. Having these defined groups has helped humanity in many ways! From storytelling, to navigation, and scientific study, there's no shortage of ways constellations have inspired us. The most popular and well-known of which is the big bear, Ursa Major!

Constellations always appear in a certain place in the sky which appears to turn around us. The path it takes and how high into the sky it gets is all determined by where you are on the Earth! In astronomy we divide the sky into two halves, the northern and southern sky. These are split up along the same line that the Earth is! We call this the celestial equator.

Ursa Major sits all the way at the top of the northern sky. Across the world many cultures depict it as a large female bear travelling along the stars.

According to the Iroquois tribe's myth, the three stars of the handle represent hunters chasing after the bear. As it drops below the horizon in fall, it shows the hunters giving up the hunt. When the bucket of the dipper disappears, the bear is caught and turns the leaves red. Then, in spring, a new bear rises from the den and the hunt begins anew!

To the Greek, Ursa Major was Hera's way of hiding the nymph Calisto from Zeus. Calisto's son, Actas, was a hunter and set out with his bow. To prevent him from shooting his mother Zeus cast him into the stars with her as Ursa Minor.

No matter the story though, Ursa Major has been a key part of navigation using the night sky! If you're far enough north it never sets below the horizon making it perfect for navigation. The two stars that make the front of the dipper point toward the north star: Polaris. It may not be the brightest in the sky, but it is invaluable for figuring out which direction you're going.

In the southern hemisphere no constellation is more appreciated than the southern cross, Crux. It bears four bright stars forming a cross which have been used for navigation and appear on many flags.

Aboriginal Australian astronomy uses Crux as a marker of the head of the Emu, not a constellation but instead an image made up of the dark spots of the Milky Way. The Yolŋu people of northern Australia saw the cross as a stingray while the Kaurna people in the south saw an eagle.

Similar to Ursa Major, Crux has also been used for navigation. In combination with Alpha and Beta Centauri, lines can be drawn mentally that cross very near to the south pole. This ability has been crucial for nighttime orientation in the southern hemisphere.

Up in the Clouds

Stars aren't the only way to see images in the sky, though! Just like the Emu, dark dust clouds in the Milky Way can hold legends as well as stars do.

The Inca found the shapes of animals in the dark patches of the Milky Way. To them, the galaxy represented a river which these celestial animals drank from. There are seven of these figures, each of them important in their own way!

The Serpent, all the way to the right, appears around the time that snakes are more active on Earth. The celestial depiction was given offerings as a way of hoping for safety from these animals.

Immediately next to the Serpent is the Toad, who appears to chase the snake out of the sky. With the Tinamou beside it, a kind of ground bird, they both represent different times of the Incan farming cycle.

Of all these figures the largest and most important was the Llama! This one contains two separate animals: the mother llama and her child. Llamas were incredibly important in Incan society as they were carriers as well as a source of food and sacrifice.

Lastly are the Fox and the Shepard. The Fox appears to be chasing after the llamas while the Shepard takes care of their flock by chasing the fox away.

Planets

What is a Planet

Whether they're made of rocks and dust or a vast collection of gas with a dense core, planets are some of the most interesting objects in the universe. Not every clump of rock or collection of gas is a planet though! Let's explore the rules that have been made to determine what is and isn't a planet.

The International Astronomical Union (IAU) set a strict definition in 2006:

1. A planet must be in orbit around its Sun
2. A planet must have enough mass to be spherical
3. A planet must clear its orbit of debris

The discovery of Eris in 2005 showed it has similar size to Pluto and would become a planet as well. This would open the door to many more planets, leading to these rules being put in place; Anything that doesn't fit these rules would instead be a dwarf planet.

This decision brought up a wide range of reactions with many being against it. Even though Pluto is now officially a dwarf planet, many people still believe it's a planet in their hearts.

A Planet's Formation

Just like stars, planets are formed when gas and dust concentrate into a dense spinning disk of debris. The majority of this (about 99.8%!) collects at the center to become the star, while everything else crashes around the outside to become everything else.

Many different kinds of objects can form in this process but planets stand out as the biggest. When a clump of rocks begins attracting more and more to it with its gravity it creates a domino effect; More rocks mean more gravity, more gravity means more rocks.

Rockies and Giants

Towards the center of the disk, where the star is, its too hot for gas to slow down or ice to form. Here we get planets like Mercury and Venus that entirely made of rock and don't have water. We call these rocky planets!

Further out is an area where ice begins to form and tags along with dust and rock. It collects in a similar way to the ones before but this time it has the ability to collect water. This is how we get our home planet, Earth.

Just a skip across the interplanetary pond is Mars! It formed similarly to Earth except that it isn't warm enough to have liquid water on the surface. There might be water underground, though, and we're still looking!

Further still in the disk it gets even colder and gas starts to slow down. At these lower speeds, the collections of rock are able to start drawing it in. Because of how light it is, gas starts to collect in enormous amounts! Jupiter and Saturn are on the larger end of these planets called gas giants.

Neptune and Uranus also count as gas giants but they're both noticeably different! They are mostly made of molecules like ammonia and methane as well as ice as rocks. These all give them their blue colors and title of ice giants!

Gravity's Tether on the Planets
You may know that Mercury is the fastest planet with one orbit taking only 3 months. Or that Pluto is by far the slowest with one orbit in 248 years. If you see a connection between their speed and distance, you're right on the mark!

If you connect a line between all the planets and the Sun and track the area that it covers is the same for each one! This property was figured out by Johannes Kepler in the 1600s. For this to be true, planets close to the Sun have to move quickly while farther ones move slowly. This is because a closer planet's orbit is shorter and has less area than a farther one.

Speed isn't the only thing that gravity can do. It can also protect us from potentially life-ending asteroids! Jupiter, being the largest planet, does this job extremely well and regularly sways the orbit of large asteroids and comets. In doing so it also ensures that Earth is completely safe from them.

Planets are also able to capture moons in the same way. One of the most common signs of a captured moon is an irregular orbit around the planet. When a moon forms along side the planet it always orbits in the same direction that the planet spins. Neptune's moon Triton on the other hand is likely to have been captured since it orbits opposite to the direction that Neptune spins.

Rogue Planets

Gravity isn't always for keeping planets in, though! Sometimes it can interact in just the right way to launch them out of the solar system. These cosmic vagabonds are called rogue planets and there's more of them out there than you might think!

Early in the Earth's formation it was hit by a Mars-sized object which knocked a lot of rock from the Earth, forming our Moon. Some planets are not so lucky; Events like this can cause planets to be ejected from their solar system!

These strange objects don't always need a star and can even form on their own. In the same way that a star is made, matter can come together to form a planet all on its own. Rogue planets formed like this are typically very large and have earned the name of sub-brown dwarfs.

Without a star you may think that these planets would be ice cold, and in most cases you'd be right! But the cosmos always has a trick up its sleeve. There is the possibility that a thick enough atmosphere or deep-sea vents could provide enough heat for life to exist. Who knows what kind of life could be out there, never feeling the warmth of a star.

Moons

What is a Moon?

When a large celestial body orbits the Sun we call it a planet, but what about when something orbits a planet? When that happens we call it a moon! There aren't many rules for that definition either, so many things can be considered a moon. Here we'll take a look at what a moon is, some of them in our solar system, and even ones outside of it!

Unlike planets, there isn't many restrictions on what a moon can be. The only solid rule is that a moon has to be a natural object. That's to say that we can't put something man-made into orbit and call it a moon.

This line can still get blurry though! Cases like the asteroid 90 Antiope or even Pluto and its moon Charon have been called a double asteroid and double planet, respectively. This is because in both of these cases there are two bodies with similar sizes that orbit each other (rather than one orbiting the other)!

The Moon in Our Sky

From lighting our sky to driving the tides of the ocean, the Moon is a key object in the night sky! Its surface tells of its violent history yet it has stood the trials of time and even helped spark life on our beautiful planet.

The Moon is thought to have been made when a Mars-sized object crashed into the Earth. This event destroyed the colliding object and ejected a massive amount of material. Eventually this material, now orbiting around the Earth, cooled down enough to form into the Moon we know today!

Large dark patches take up a lot of space on the Moon's surface. These are called maria which means "seas" in Latin. Although we know now that these patches are made up of dark rock called basalt, early astronomers mistook them to be actual oceans!

You may also know that the Moon is covered in tons of craters. These are caused when a large object, like an asteroid, collides into the moon and leaves a hole on impact. The brightest of these craters is called Tycho after the astronomer Tycho Brahe and can be found in the lower left portion of the Moon.

It's important that the Moon formed too: All of life depends on the existence of the Moon. In the beginning life did alright on its own existing around deep-sea vents. But as it became more complex, and needed more nutrients, it began to rely on the currents of the ocean. Without the Moon there would be no currents, and that means no life.

Moons of the Solar System

Although our Moon is beautiful and important, it isn't the only one in the solar system; In fact, it's far from being the only one! Every planet besides Mercury and Venus has a moon. While most of these are just small fragments of rock and ice, there are also some incredible exceptions!

Mars has two small moons which orbit very close to it compared to Earth's moon. They are called Phobos and Deimos which mean "fear" and "terror" in Greek. Fitting names for Mars, named after the Roman god of war! They aren't forever though, Phobos is likely to be torn apart and will crash into Mars in the distant future.

Jupiter has 79 known moons orbiting around it, the four largest of these moons are called the Galilean moons. The first of these is called Io and boasts a bright yellow surface caused by volcanic activity. Europa is next, it has intricately crossing lines across it and may even harbor life under its surface! The third and most massive moon is Ganymede, it is the only known moon in the solar system to have its own magnetic field. The furthest one out, Callisto, is also the darkest of them all and has an incredibly high density of craters.

With 82 known moon, Saturn has the most moons of all the planets. The most well known of these is called Titan though there are also other large ones such as Rhea and Enceladus. Although it has not been confirmed, there is evidence that Rhea could have a thin ring system made up of tiny particles of rock! Enceladus is almost completely covered in fresh ice which is produced by cryovolcanoes that eject the material from beneath the surface.

Uranus has 27 known moons, five of those are major moons with Titania being the largest. Its surface has a reddish color which is likely caused by the moon collecting colored material from Uranus' moon system. This is contrasted by newer impact craters which shower a bluer surface color.

Neptune has the least number of moons among the gas giants with only 14 known moons. The largest of these are Triton, which orbits backwards, and Proteus. Similar to Enceladus, Triton has cryovolcanoes that shoot out water and ammonia rather than lava. This makes its surface relatively young and free of craters!

Even dwarf planets can have moons! Pluto has five, the largest being Charon, with all of their names relating to the Greek underworld. Eris, named after the Roman goddess of discord, has one moon called Dysnomia which means "anarchy" in Greek. The outer solar system truly is dark, both of light and in name!

Europa and Titan
Of all the moons in the solar system there are three which stand out: Europa and Titan. Both of them seem very different from each other but they do share one thing in common. That is the possibility of harboring life!

Europa has long stood as a place to look for life in our solar system. Its frozen and cracked surface likely holds a liquid ocean of water underneath it. Not every planet with water has an ocean like this, though, so what sets it apart? The answer is tidal heating.

The push and pull on Europa from Jupiter and the other Galilean moons cause the rock and ice that make it to stretch. This stretching then relaxes and releases heat into the planet in a process called tidal heating. This could release enough energy to keep an entire ocean from freezing! With a planet-wide ocean of liquid water there is surely a chance that life could be thriving underneath the surface.

Though it may also have an ocean below its surface, Titan's claim to fame is right at the surface. The moon has entire lakes of molecules called hydrocarbons like methane which could support life but not as we know it! If life were to exist here it would inhale hydrogen instead of oxygen and exhale methane instead of carbon dioxide.

This life not-as-we-know-it would face a great challenge, though: temperature. You may know how hard it feels to move when you're really cold but imagine how difficult it would be at -290 degrees Fahrenheit! It may seem hopeless but with just the right conditions life could survive even that.

Exomoons

It stands to reason that exoplanets could also have moons. Although none have been confirmed yet we still have a name for them: exomoons!

The exoplanet HD 189733 b is one of the likely candidates to have a moon based on the spectra we see from it. The moon is suspected to be similar to Io based on the amount of sodium and potassium that we can detect near to the planet. Exomoons like this are also called an Exo-Io!

The most used way to find these moons, though, is by looking for how a potential moon dims the light of its star. This is also how exoplanets can be found which makes it difficult to distinguish, especially since moons are often much smaller than their planet.

A Star's Aftermath

Death of a Star

Every star of every kind will eventually run out of fuel. When it does the result can be anything from just fizzling out to creating the most destructive force in the universe.

No matter which one you choose the death of a star starts with one event: running out of hydrogen. Eventually a star will have fused nearly all of its hydrogen into helium. When this happens there isn't enough energy to fight against the gravity of the star. The star begins to collapse into itself and then one of two things happens.

If the star is like our Sun it will start collapse on itself and provide enough pressure to fuse heavier elements. As this happens it begins to shed its fuel into space and grow much bigger in size. At this point it is called a red giant star!

As the red giant burns through the last of its fuel it sheds what's left of it in a relatively gentle process. These create planetary nebula which are named for their resemblance to planets to early astronomers.

With stars much larger than our Sun though it's a different story. The star begins to collapse in the same way only this time there's more mass behind it. As the pressure builds heavier elements start fusing, but it doesn't stop there!

The star continues to crush everything towards its core until it reaches a specific point. Under enough pressure the star implodes as a supernova and releases an extreme amount of energy! What's left behind is the nebulous remains of the star in a supernova remnant.

White Dwarfs

At the center of every planetary nebula is a white dwarf. White dwarfs are unusually dim for stars with most being too dim to see with the naked eye. This is because they're not stars, not really. Instead they're more like the left over core of a star.

The light that these bodies give off isn't from the fusing of hydrogen anymore. All of it has been compacted down so heavily that it can't be used in that way. Instead, all of the light given off is entirely from the left over heat of the star.

When a white dwarf eventually radiates all of its heat away it will grow dimmer until it is entirely cooled down. At this point it gives off no more light and becomes a black dwarf. With no more reactions happening it's thought that these will be some of the longest lasting objects in the cosmos.

Neutron Stars
When every massive star goes supernova there are two distinct outcomes that depend entirely on how big the star is. Though its much less destructive, the outcome for smaller stars is still awe inspiring. They're called neutron stars and just like it says in the name, they're made of the extremely dense neutrons from atoms.

To get an idea of how compressed these stars are, imagine the white dwarf from before. It has the mass of the Sun in a small Earth-sized package.

A neutron star takes that same amount of mass and squeezes it even further. All of this star stuff is compacted into the size of a city!

Black Holes
The most destructive, powerful, and dense object in the entire cosmos: a black hole.

The death of an extremely massive star is so powerful that it can literally break the universe. As the star collapses on itself, the extreme amount of mass continues to push down on it far beyond the point of a neutron star. It quickly reaches the point of no return where gravity becomes so strong that nothing can stop it!

In place of a giant star is now a point in space that is infinitely compressed called a singularity. If that sounds confusing, don't worry! Black holes are one of the least understood objects in the cosmos. And that isn't helped by their gravity being strong enough to keep even light from escaping!

See It For Yourself

The cosmos has so many treasures hidden deep within it, but so many of these are too far away to see yourself. That's okay though! There are plenty of beautiful shows on the cosmic stage that we can see right from Earth and without a telescope.

Whether you're in the northern or southern hemisphere, there's almost always something going on in the sky! We'll look at several events in both here so no matter where you are you'll have a treasure to look forward to.

Meteor Showers

When small pieces of an asteroid or comet travel into Earth's path they crash through the sky making a bright streak. When these pieces are entirely burned up in the atmosphere they're called meteors; A group of these is the wonderful display of light we call a meteor shower!

All throughout the year the Earth passes through the orbits of tiny bits of rock and dust in annual meteor showers. We categorize these showers based on the time of year that they show up and what constellation they appear in. The Eta Aquariids, for example, show up in May and appear to come from the constellation Aquarius!

For January, the northern sky is the place to look for these beautiful showers. From late December through mid January is the Quadrantids in the constellation Boötes! You'll find many of these meteors coming from just below the Big Dipper.

Just to the right of these are the Gamma Ursae Minorids in Ursa Minor! They're most active from mid to late January where you'll find them coming near the bottom of the dipper.

The southern sky gets its debut through February and March. In the constellation Centaurus are the Alpha Centaurids that appear from the end of January to mid February. They come right at the top of the constellation near Alpha Centauri.

The Gamma Normids appear for almost an entire month from mid February to mid March! These meteors come from the constellation Norma, meaning "normal" in Latin. It represents the right angle of a carpenter's ruler.

April brings us a mix of northern and southern sky showers. In the north there is the Lyrids which rain down from mid to late April. You'll find them in the constellation Lyra near its brightest star, Vega.

The Eta Aquariids in the southern sky is one of the most fascinating meteor showers of the year! It appears from mid April to late May in the constellation Aquarius. The debris that causes this meteor shower comes from the famous Halley's Comet!

Through early to mid May are the Eta Lyrids which come from the constellation Lyra. Although they're close in time and come from the same place, this shower and the April Lyrids actually come from different comets!

As their name implies, the June Boötids occur from mid June to early July. These meteors come from the northern constellation Boötes. You'll find this shower near the head of the constellation.

From early July through mid August there are the Alpha Capricornids in the southern sky. Although it has a low rate of meteors per hour now this shower is expected to be stronger than any one we've seen 200 years from now!

Through late August and early September are the Augrigids in the northern constellation Auriga, the chariot driver. Then in October are the Orionids which are also meteors that come from Halley's Comet.

Last but far from the least is the many showers that appear through November and December. There are too many to list here so instead we'll look at the most impressive ones. The Leonids are active throughout November and boast bright meteors which have been recorded throughout history.

The December Ursids radiate from just below the Little Dipper. Being so high in the sky, this shower is in a perfect position for stargazing. Not only can you see it even above trees, it's also well placed for laying down and looking at the stars.

The Moon
Of everything in the night sky, our Moon is by far the brightest. Even when the Moon is at its absolute dimmest it is still brighter than the brightest star.

This makes it perfect for stargazing with the naked eye. Not only is it bright, there are also a wide array of lunar events you can look for!

The lunar phases are perhaps the best way of getting to know the moon. Once you learn them they're easy to remember and it can be a fun challenge to go stargazing and see if you can tell what phase its in!

The first phase of the lunar cycle is the New Moon. At this point the Moon is on the same side of the Sun and fully within its own shadow. The Sun is usually too bright and completely drowns out this phase—If you've ever thought that the Moon was missing, this is probably why!

Next are the waxing phases of the Moon. In this case the word "waxing" means to be growing because in these phases the Moon is appearing to become bigger. You'll likely see a Waxing Crescent during the day at some point since the Moon hasn't moved far enough from the Sun yet.

The next phase is called the First Quarter. It may seem like it should be called the first half since half of the Moon is shining. The reason it isn't is because we only ever see one half of the Moon and a half of a half is a quarter.

A Waxing Gibbous, the next phase, gets its name from Latin and means "humped" or "bent". As this phase gets bigger it can get harder to tell if the Moon is full or not.

The Full Moon is by far one of the most beautiful events in the night sky. With an entire half of the Moon's surface reflecting light down to Earth it can bright enough to cast a shadow. This phase is also the only time that a lunar eclipse can happen!

A lunar eclipse is when the full Moon is in the shadow of the Earth. When this happens the Moon can look like it's orange or even a deep red. This is because longer wavelengths of light like red and orange more easily pass through our atmosphere. This light then bounces off of the Moon and back down to Earth, coloring it red!

The other side of the lunar phases is the waning phases. As the opposite to waxing, "waning" means to fade or shrink. As the Moon appears to shrink it goes through the Waning Gibbous, the Last Quarter, the Waning Crescent, and finally back to a new Moon.

New Moons also have a special event associated with them that you may have already seen: a solar eclipse!

Solar Eclipses

A solar eclipse occurs when the Moon is in just the right position to block out some or even all of the Sun. Since this needs a new Moon to happen you might wonder why we don't have them every month. There is one thing that determines everything about a solar eclipse: the tilt of the Moon's orbit.

Imagine the Sun and all of the planets as being on a disk. The Earth orbits along this disk but the Moon is on its own slightly tilted disk. If they were both aligned we would see a solar eclipse every month as the Moon blocked out the Sun. But because of its tilt it only lines up perfectly on rare occasions.

When the Moon aligns perfectly with the Sun it completely blocks it out in what's called a total solar eclipse. Watching this happen in person feels almost unreal. The Sun turns black, the air becomes cold, and the birds stop chirping.

This difference in angle also means that the Moon isn't always big enough in the sky to block out the Sun entirely. In this case one of two things happen: an annular or partial solar eclipse.

An annular solar eclipse is when the Moon is centered on the Sun but it isn't big enough to fully block it out. It instead makes the Sun appear like a ring around the Moon. The name itself comes from the Latin word anularis meaning "ring-shaped".

The Moon isn't always centered though and sometimes it will only block out a portion of the Sun. In a partial solar eclipse it looks like a huge bite has been taken out of the Sun.

There's still one more type of solar eclipse though it is much rarer. It's called a hybrid solar eclipse! These happen when a solar eclipse starts as a total eclipse in one part of the world. As the Moon moves across the sky though it moves far enough away that the eclipse becomes an annular one in another part of the world!

Comets

Comets are a common but still unforgettable appearance in the night sky. These clumps of rock and ice begin to melt and release gases which we call the tail of the comet. This tail gets bigger and bigger until the comet gets to the closest point in its orbit around the Sun! As beautifully as it began the tail dies out until it comes back around.

What makes these events seem so rare though is their brightness. Even though there are plenty of comets visible from Earth at any given time, most of them are only bright enough to see with a telescope. Still, there are plenty of bright ones for years to come if you have the patience to wait for them!

Glossary

A

Alpha Capricornids: A meteor shower that occurs from July 15th to August 10th in the constellation Capricornus.

Alpha Centauri: The closest star system to our Sun, it is a triple system composed of A, B, and C. The third one is also called Proxima Centauri, an M-type red dwarf.

Alpha Centaurids: A meteor shower in the constellation Centaurus from around January 31st to February 20th.

ammonia: A molecule with the formula NH_3, it is found almost everywhere in the solar system and causes Uranus' and Neptune's blue color.

Andromeda Galaxy: The nearest spiral galaxy to the Milky Way, it is one of the only galaxies visible to the naked eye. In about four billion years it will collide with the Milky Way and form a galaxy called Milkdromeda.

Annie Cannon: An astronomer who studied at Radcliffe College with Edward Pickering. She was crucial to classifying large amounts of cataloged stars.

annular solar eclipse: A solar eclipse where the Moon is centered on the Sun but isn't big enough to fully block it out, forming a ring.

90 Antiope: A double asteroid made up of two nearly equally sized asteroids orbiting each other.

Aquarius: A constellation in the southern sky, its name means "water carrier" in Latin. It contains the G-type star Sadalsuud.

Arcturus: The brightest star in the constellation Boötes, it is a K-type red giant.

asteroid: A celestial body in the solar system that orbits the Sun and isn't large enough to form itself into a sphere.

averted vision: A method of seeing dimmer objects in the night sky by looking slightly to the side of them.

B

basalt: A type of igneous rock that causes the dark color of marias on the Moon.

Bayer designation: A method of classifying stars based on brightness using Greek letters and the constellation the star is in.

black dwarf: A white dwarf that has cooled down and no longer emits visible light.

black hole: An object so massive that even light cannot escape it, it is the result of a giant star dying.

blackbody: An object which perfectly absorbs all light that hits it.

Boötes: A constellation in the northern sky, its name comes from the Greek for "ox-driver". It contains the K-type star Arcturus.

brown dwarf: A sub-stellar object that isn't massive enough to fuse hydrogen into helium.

C

Callisto: Jupiter's second largest moon, it has the oldest and most cratered surface in the solar system.

Canis Minor: A constellation in the northern sky, its name is Latin for "lesser dog". It contains the F-type star Procyon.

catadioptric: The use of both reflecting mirrors and refracting lenses.

celestial equator: An imaginary line in the sky above the Earth's equator that divides the sky into two halves.

Centaurus: A constellation in the southern sky, it represents a centaur, a Greek myth of a half human, half horse. It contains the G-type star Alpha Centauri.

Charon: Pluto's largest moon, it has also been considered as a double planet because it and Pluto orbit each other.

comet: A celestial body made primarily of ice that melts and releases a trail of gas when it gets near to the Sun.

constellation: A collection of bright stars that depicts a figure, often one based in mythology. There are 88 official ones as defined by the IAU.

Corvus: A constellation in the southern sky, its name comes from the Latin for "crow". It contains the B-type star Gienah.

cosmic microwave background radiation: Left over radiation from the Big Bang that lets us study the ancient universe.

Crux: A constellation in the southern sky, its name comes from the Latin for "cross". It contains the B-type star Acrux.

cryovolcano: A kind of volcano that erupts with liquids like water or methane instead of lava.

D

dark matter: Mysterious matter that only interacts through gravity.

Deimos: The smallest of Mars' two moons, its name means "dread" in Greek.

double asteroid: A binary system that occurs when two asteroids are orbiting each other.

double planet: A binary system that occurs when two planets are orbiting each other.

dwarf planet: A planetary body in the solar system that doesn't meet all three of the IAU's rules for a planet.

Dysnomia: Eris' only known moon, its name means "anarchy" in Greek.

E

Earth: The third planet from the Sun, it is a rocky planet and host to all known life.

Edward Pickering: An astronomer who studied at Harvard and discovered binary stars using their spectra.

electro-magnetic spectrum: The spectrum of light separated by their wavelengths. This is the way we observe everything in the universe.

Emu in the Sky: A large dark patch in the Milky Way seen as an Emu in Aboriginal Australian astronomy. It is important for its apparent match to the life cycle of emus on Earth.

Enceladus: Saturn's sixth largest moon, the ice that covers it makes it one of the most reflective moons in the solar system.

Eris: The second-largest dwarf planet and one of the most distant natural objects from the Sun.

Eta Aquariids: A meteor shower in the southern sky occurring from around April 19th to May 28th in the constellation Aquarius. The meteors come from the famous comet, Halley's Comet.

Eta Lyrids: A meteor shower in the northern sky occurring from around May 3rd to May 14th in the constellation Lyra.

Europa: The smallest of Jupiter's Galilean moons, it has an incredibly smooth surface which is likely supported by an ocean below the surface.

Exo-Io: An exomoon which closely matches the features of Jupiter's moon, Io.

exomoon: A moon of an exoplanet.

eyepiece: A set of lenses that focuses light from a telescope onto your eye.

F

F-type star: Stars with temperatures around 7,000K and a little more mass than the Sun. Examples of this type are Procyon and Gamma Virginis.

first quarter: The third lunar phase, it is exactly 50-percent full and will continue to grow.

Flamsteed designation: A way of classifying stars based on position using numbers and the constellation the star is in.

full Moon: The fifth lunar phase when the Moon is opposite from the Sun and fully lit.

fusion: The process of hydrogen merging with three other hydrogens to form helium, releasing enormous amounts of energy in the process.

G

G-type star: Stars with temperatures around 6,000K and similar masses to the Sun. Examples of this type are our own Sun and Alpha Centauri.

Galilean moons: The four largest moons of Jupiter discovered by Galileo in the 1600s.

Gamma Corvi: Also called Gienah, it is a B-type star and the brightest one in the constellation Corvus.

Gamma Normids: A meteor shower in the southern sky occurring around March 7th to March 23rd in the constellation Norma.

gamma ray: A photon with immense amounts of energy, they have wavelengths even shorter than the size of singular atoms. They are produced by events like dying stars and black holes consuming entire stars.

Gamma Ursae Minorids: A meteor shower that occurs from January 10th to January 22nd in the constellation Ursa Minor.

Ganymede: The largest of Jupiter's Galilean moons, it is the only moon in the solar system to have a magnetic field and is larger than Mercury.

gas giant: A type of planet consisting of a small rocky core surrounded by a vast amount of gasses like hydrogen, helium, and ammonia.

GPS: The Global Positioning System, a joint effort of satellites that allows anyone to know exactly where they are on the Earth.

gravitational wave: A ripple in the fabric of space caused by powerful events such as the merging of black holes.

H

H-R Diagram: A graph that maps and classifies stars by their temperature and brightness.

HD 189733 b: An exoplanet 64 light-years away from Earth, it is slightly larger than Jupiter and orbits around its star every 2.2 days.

Halley's Comet: A famous comet which is visible from Earth every 75 years.

Hubble Space Telescope: A visible light space telescope that was launched in 1990 and continues to operate today. It has been crucial in learning about and understanding the cosmos.

hybrid solar eclipse:

hydrocarbon: A molecule that only contains hydrogen and carbon, these molecules appear on many different bodies in the solar system.

hydrogen: The first element of the periodic table, it consists of a single proton and electron.

I

ice giant: A type of gas giant with a core made of ices and rock. Their atmospheres typically contain less hydrogen and helium than typical gas giants.

infrared: A low energy photon just below red on the visible spectrum. It is produced by almost everything that gives off heat and is important to finding brown dwarfs.

International Astronomical Union: An organization focusing on the science of astronomy that meets to do many things including naming celestial bodies.

Io: The third largest of Jupiter's Galilean moons, it is extremely volcanic which causes its surface to be a bright yellow.

J

James Webb Space Telescope: Also called JWST or Webby, this space telescope is set to be the successor to Hubble. It will see in the infrared spectrum with incredible sensitivity.

Johannes Kepler: A German astronomer who lived in the 17th century, he was important in the discovery of how the planets actually moved in the solar system.

June Boötids: A meteor shower that occurs from June 22nd to July 2nd in the constellation Boötes.

Jupiter: The fifth planet from the sun, it is a gas giant and the largest planet in the solar system.

K

K-type star: Stars with temperatures around 4,000K and masses about half that of the Sun. Examples of this type are Arcturus and Pollux.

L

L-type dwarf: Brown dwarfs with temperatures around 2,000K without the mass necessary to fuse hydrogen. Examples of this type are V838 Monocerotis and GD 165.

Large Ultraviolet Optical Infrared Surveyor: Also called LUVOIR, it is a planned space telescope that will be over twice as large as the JWST. Its main goal is to find and categorize exoplanets.

Laser Interferometer Space Antenna: Also called LISA, this planned space probe will orbit the Sun and detect gravitational waves with incredible accuracy. It is set to launch in the year 2034.

last quarter: The seventh lunar phase, it is a distinct point of 50-percent illumination that will then shrink.

Leonids: A meteor shower that occurs from November 6th to November 30th in the constellation Leo.

lunar eclipse: When the Earth blocks out the Sun as the Moon moves into the Earth's shadow as it orbits.

Lyra: A constellation in the northern sky, its name is Greek for "lyre", a kind of musical instrument. It contains the A-type star Vega.

Lyrids: A meteor shower in the northern sky that occurs around April 16th to April 26th in the constellation Lyra.

M

magnitude: A scale for the brightness of stars where a lower number means a brighter star.

maria: Large regions of dark basalt on the Moon. They were named after the Latin word for "seas" because of their appearance.

Mars: The fourth planet from the Sun, it is a rocky planet with a distinctly red color giving it the title of "The Red Planet".

Mercury: The closest planet to the Sun, it is a rocky planet that orbits incredibly quickly with a full orbit taking only 3 months.

meteor: Any piece of natural space debris that falls to Earth and burns up in the atmosphere.

meteor shower: An event in the night sky where multiple meteors appear to come from the same point in the sky.

methane: A molecule with the formula CH_4, it is mostly found on Earth but can also be found in Uranus and Neptune which gives them their blue color.

microwave: A low energy photon with wavelengths about as long as these letters. They make up the cosmic microwave background.

Moon: Earth's moon and only natural satellite, compared to other moons it has an unusually big size compared to its planet.

moon: A celestial body in the solar system that orbits a planet or other body.

N

naked-eye astronomy: Viewing the night sky without the aid of a telescope or other instrument.

nebula: Massive clouds of dust and gas that can fuel the formation of stars. They can be made by the death of stars.

Neptune: The farthest planet from the Sun, it is an ice giant and the densest of all the gas giants.

neutron star: The core of a massive star which collapsed but wasn't big enough to form a black hole.

new Moon: The first phase of the lunar cycle, the Moon is on the same side of the Earth as the Sun and so it is completely dark.

Norma: A constellation in the southern sky, it means "normal" in Latin and represents the right angle of a carpenter's ruler.

northern sky: The top half of the sky as divided by the celestial equator.

nova: The explosion of a star when it runs out of fuel to burn and collapses in on itself.

O

Orionids: A meteor shower that occurs from October 2nd to November 7th in the constellation Orion.

P

Phobos: The largest of Mars' two moons, its name means "fear" in Greek.

photon: A type of particle/wave produced by almost everything in the universe. It is the carrier of every wave on the electro-magnetic spectrum.

planet: A celestial body that orbits a star, is big enough to be spherical, and has cleared its orbit of other objects.

planetary nebula: A nebula formed by the death of a star like the Sun shedding its mass.

Pluto: A former planet and now a dwarf planet, it is made of rock and ice and has a heart-shaped glacier made of frozen nitrogen.

Polaris: The current closest star to the celestial north pole, it is an F-type star and the brightest one in Ursa Minor.

potassium: The nineteenth element of the periodic table, its spectra can be used to detect exomoons similar to Io.

probe: A machine that we put into space specialized to collect specific types of data.

Procyon: The brightest star in the constellation Canis Minor, it is an F-type main sequence stars. At 11.46 light-years away, it is one of the closest stars to the Sun.

Proteus: Neptune's second largest moon, due to its irregular shape it is likely a captured asteroid.

Proxima Centauri: The third and dimmest star of the Alpha Centauri system. It is an M-type red dwarf and is the closest star to the Sun at 4.24 light-years away.

Q

Quadrantids: A meteor shower in the northern sky that occurs around December 28th to January 12th.

quasar: An incredibly bright center of a galaxy that puts out radiation across the entire electro-magnetic spectrum.

<h1 style="text-align:center">R</h1>

radio wave: A low energy photon with the longest wavelengths of the electro-magnetic spectrum. They can have wavelengths as long as football field.

red giant: A Sun-like star that has used up the majority of its fuel but has grown up to 200 times the size of the Sun.

reflection: The property of a material that bounces light away from it at the same angle it hit it with.

refraction: The property of a material that changes the direction of light when it passes through it.

Rhea: Saturn's second largest moon, under the right conditions it could have an ocean below its surface.

rocky planet: A planet composed mostly of rocks and metals and have a defined surface unlike gas giants.

rogue planet: A planet without a host star. They are often thrown from their solar system but can also form on their own.

<h1 style="text-align:center">S</h1>

Saturn: The sixth planet from the Sun and the second-largest planet in the solar system. It is a gas giant with a remarkable ring system that can be seen from Earth with a telescope.

singularity: The core of a black hole, a reality-tearing point of infinite density.

Sirius: The brightest star in the night sky, it is a main sequence A-type star. Its name comes from the Greek word *seírios*, meaning "scorching".

sodium: The eleventh element of the periodic table, its spectra can be used to find exomoons like Io.

southern sky: The southern half of the sky as divided by the celestial equator.

solar eclipse: When the Moon passes in front of the Sun and blocks some or all of its light.

southern sky: The night sky as seen from the southern hemisphere of Earth.

spectra: The wavelengths of light given off by a star.

spectral type: The classification of stars based on their spectra and temperature.

sub-brown dwarf: A body in the cosmos which is much larger than Jupiter but not enough to be considered a brown dwarf.

Sun: The star that supports all life on Earth and holds the entire solar system together. Without it neither Earth nor any of the planets would exist.

supernova: An extremely powerful explosion caused by the collapse of a giant star.

supernova remnant: The nebula that a supernova forms that will continue to expand as matter explodes outward.

T

T-type dwarf: Brown dwarfs with temperatures around 1,000K without the mass to fuse hydrogen. Examples of this type are Gliese 229b and HN Pegasi B.

tidal heating: The heating of a celestial body by the push and pull of gravity.

Titan: Saturn's largest moon and the second-largest moon in the solar system, it is the only moon found to have a liquid at its surface.

Titania: Uranus' largest moon, it has a slightly red color due to debris from other bodies in the solar system.

total solar eclipse: A solar eclipse where the Moon completely blocks out the Sun.

Triangulum: A constellation in the northern sky, its name means triangle in Latin.

Triangulum Galaxy: A spiral galaxy 2.7 million light-years away from Earth and one of the only galaxies visible to the naked eye. It can be found in the northern constellation, Triangulum.

Triton: Neptune's largest moon, it has a retrograde orbit around Neptune and is thought to be a dwarf planet that the planet captured.

Tycho: One of the largest craters on the moon, it is named after the astronomer Tycho Brahe.

Tycho Brahe: A Danish astronomer who was important in charting supernovae and describing how the Moon orbited the Earth.

U

ultraviolet: Light with wavelengths about the size of a virus, it is produced heavily by the Sun and is what causes sunburns.

Uranus: The seventh planet from the Sun, it is a gas giant mainly composed of hydrogen and helium. The cyan color of it is from methane in its atmosphere that absorbs a lot of red light.

Ursa Major: A constellation in the northern sky, its name means "greater she-bear" in Latin and contains the famous asterism the Big Dipper.

Ursids: A meteor shower that occurs between December 17th and December 26th in the constellation Ursa Minor.

V

Vega: The brightest star in the constellation Lyra. It is an A-type star and one of the closest ones to Earth, being 25 light-years away.

Venus: The second planet from the Sun, it is a rocky planet with a densely clouded atmosphere that rains sulfuric acid.

visible light: The spectrum of light that we see the universe with. It is easily transmitted by the atmosphere, allowing us to observe space from the Earth.

W

waning crescent: The eighth lunar phase, it shrinks from being 50- to 0-percent full.

waning gibbous: The sixth lunar phase, it shrinks from being 100- to 50-percent full.

wavelength: The width of a wave of light, longer wavelengths have less energy while shorter ones have more.

waxing crescent: The second lunar phase, it grows from being 0- to 50-percent full.

waxing gibbous: The fourth lunar phase, it grows from being 50- to 100-percent full.

white dwarf: The left over core of a Sun-mass star that has run out of fuel.

X

x-ray: High-energy photons with wavelengths about as wide as an atom. They are produced by objects like pulsars and black holes.

www.ingramcontent.com/pod-product-compliance
Lightning Source LLC
Chambersburg PA
CBHW071313130726
47997CB00007B/2540